A Children's
Guide to Worship

by

Ruth L. Boling, Lauren J. Muzzy, Laurie A. Vance

illustrated by
Tracey Dahle Carrier

Geneva Press
Louisville, Kentucky

Published by Geneva Press
Louisville, Kentucky

This book is printed on acid-free paper that meets the
American National Standards Institute Z39.48 standard. ∞

PRINTED IN THE UNITED STATES OF AMERICA
99 00 01 02 03 04 05 06 — 10 9 8 7 6 5 4

ISBN 0-664-50015-3

In Memoriam

A Children's Guide to Worship is dedicated
by The Rev. Harold G. and Joan N. Williams
to the glory of God and in loving memory of
Miriam L. Noll,
who as a mother and teacher nurtured children
throughout her life.

With parents as partners, each church is called to nurture children in their commitment to Christ and community, through scripture study, stewardship, worship, fellowship, and Christian caring.

Welcome to Worship
A Guide for Children, Families, and Friends

Message to Parents

The Sunday service is a community activity during which all God's people gather as one to worship. This includes singing to God, praying to God, hearing God's Word, and giving to God. In addition, this includes two special acts of worship that occur from time to time and are featured on two special pages in this booklet. They are the Sacrament of Baptism and the Sacrament of Holy Communion. Children belong in our worship services simply by virtue of their baptisms. However, children need help in understanding the service so they can worship God meaningfully.

At home, children learn appropriate table manners by eating together with the family, night after night. Eventually the family reaps the benefits: mealtimes become more meaningful, ordered gatherings—true family time. In the same way, children learn to worship by worshiping! This will happen over time, through regular attendance and strong parental support.

This *Guide to Worship* is offered in order that you—the primary Christian educators of your children—may introduce them to the life-changing, wonderful discipline of Christian worship.

Assemble in God's Name

Hello, children. We welcome you here this morning! You belong to God's family, and we are glad you have come to worship God with us. This morning we will worship God in many different ways. However, there are four "regular acts of worship" that we will use the most. They are:

1. We hear God's Word.	2. We sing to God.	3. We pray to God.	4. We give to God.

As you turn the pages, you will see that worship follows a definite plan every Sunday. The church mice on every page will help you follow this plan.

God is very pleased with us when we worship together. We are all children of God.

Prelude

As we gather to worship God, the beautiful organ music helps us feel closer to God. Look around to see what is special about today's service.

Are we sharing communion today?
Are we having a baptism today?
Which choir will be singing today?
Can you tell what season of the church year we are in?
Can you find the first hymn in your hymnal?

Call to Worship

We stand and share words that invite us to begin worshiping God.

Hymn of Praise

We stand and sing a joyful song to praise our God.
Hooray for God!

Prayer of the Day

We begin with a prayer to tell God how much we adore God. Sometimes this prayer reminds us of something special about God that we are celebrating today.

Call to Confession

Nobody's perfect. God knows that. God asks us to admit our faults, using the Prayer of Confession.

Prayer of Confession

We try to follow God and do the right thing. But when we don't, we can ask God to forgive us. We try to help all the people in God's world. But when we don't do enough, we can tell God we are sorry. This is what "confession" means.

Personal Confession

Use this quiet time to tell God anything else you are sorry for. To end our prayer, we say "AMEN," which means "so be it." Watch for other places where we say "AMEN" in worship.

Declaration of Forgiveness

After saying we are sorry, we hear the good news that God forgives us for everything. **Thanks be to God!**

Gloria Patri

We now stand and sing because we are happy that God has forgiven us. "Gloria Patri" means "Glory to the Father." This has been sung by Christians for nearly 2,000 years.

> "Glory be to the Father,
> And to the Son,
> And to the Holy Ghost;
> As it was in the beginning,
> Is now, and ever shall be,
> World without end.
> Amen. Amen."

Apostles' Creed*

We say together what we believe as a church family. Can you find the Apostles' Creed in your hymnal? What can you learn from the Apostles' Creed about God, Jesus, the Holy Ghost, and the Church? Sometimes we use different words to say what we believe. When we do, this is called an "Affirmation of Faith."

*Some churches do this later in the service, after the sermon. What does your church do?

Children's Message

Come forward with the other children to hear a story about God's love for us.

The Sacrament of Baptism

Sometimes we have a baptism. Through baptism, a baby, child, or adult becomes a member of God's family, the Church. We promise to help this person grow to know God's love. **This is a special day**. Can you think of something YOU can do to welcome this person to our church family?

Proclaim God's Word

Anthem

The choir sings a song that helps us worship. How does this music make you feel? What do the words say about God?

Prayer for Illumination

In this prayer we ask the Holy Spirit to help us understand God's Word the Bible. "Illumination" means "turning the light on." When we understand something from the Bible for the very first time, it can feel like somebody turned the light on for us! Do you feel that way?

Scripture Reading

God's Word is written in the scriptures. Listen very carefully! Can you find today's scripture readings in the Bible? The readings can be from the Old Testament (front of the Bible) or the New Testament (back of the Bible).

Sermon   *The Word Preached*

Our pastor talks about what the scripture readings mean. We can learn about God's love for us. We can also learn how God wants us to live today. Ask God to help you listen to the sermon.

Apostles' Creed

Some churches say the Apostles' Creed now. When our pastor finishes the sermon, it is our turn to say what we believe. Imagine that YOU are a pastor giving a short sermon when you stand and say these important words.

Hymn of Response

We stand and sing another hymn. Does the hymn remind you of anything you just heard in the scripture readings or the sermon?

Prayers of Thanksgiving, Petition, and Intercession

First we share our joys and concerns with each other. Then the pastor leads a prayer that has three parts:

1. Thanksgiving - Thanking God
2. Petition - Asking God to help us
3. Intercession - Asking God to help others

The Lord's Prayer

Now we say together the special prayer that Jesus taught his disciples.

"Our Father who art in heaven,
Hallowed be Thy name.
Thy Kingdom come,
Thy will be done,
On Earth
As it is in Heaven.
Give us this day our daily bread;
And forgive us our debts,
As we forgive our debtors;
And lead us not into temptation,
But deliver us from evil.
For Thine is the Kingdom
And the power
And the glory, forever.
Amen."

Ministry of Peace

We share the peace of God's love with God's family. We can say, "Peace be with you." We can respond, "And also with you."

THIS DO IN REMEMBRANCE OF ME

The Sacrament of Holy Communion

Holy Communion, or the Lord's Supper, is a joyous event celebrated by Christians everywhere.
Through the Lord's Supper, we

- Give thanks to God
- Remember Jesus
- Celebrate Jesus giving his life for us
- Celebrate our togetherness

The pastor tells us about Jesus and the last meal he shared with his disciples.

What is special to you about the Lord's Supper?

Go in God's Name

Offering

Our gifts support the work of the church. We give our time, our talents, and our money. *We give our selves*. We give to God because God gives so much to us. Everything we have comes from God. Listen to the offering music and think about that!

Doxology

This is a Greek word meaning "to give God glory."

> "Praise God from whom all blessings flow;
> Praise Him*, all creatures here below;
> Praise Him* above, ye heavenly host:
> Praise Father, Son, and Holy Ghost. Amen."
> *or "God"

Prayer of Dedication

The ushers bring our gifts forward to God.
Together we pray God will help us use these gifts to do God's work.

Imagine where your gifts will end up!

Closing Hymn

Find the correct page in the hymnal.

Benediction and Postlude

At the end of the service, we stand and listen
to the benediction, which means "good word."

The "good word" is that God goes with us into
the world to do God's work.

We listen to joyful music as we go. We go to
love others just as God loves us.

Afterword
How "A Children's Guide to Worship" Came to Be

"Are we having communion today?" asked Anna, age seven and a half.
"Yes," whispered her mother, "how can you tell?"
"I can smell it," said Anna.

"I *love* wearing my Cherub Choir robe," said Lauren at age five. "It makes me feel just like a minister."

On the way home from church William and Mariel (ages eleven and nine) requested spaghetti and chocolate cake for supper. Spaghetti and chocolate cake had been mentioned in the Children's Message that morning during worship. Their mother agreed, on the condition that the children tell their father the whole story, as they remembered it, at the supper table.

"Our Lord Jesus Christ took bread and after giving thanks he broke it, and gave it to his disciples saying, 'This bread is my body, broken for you. Take, eat. Do this in remembrance of me,'" said Allison, at age seven, reciting the Words of Institution verbatim and lifting a leftover hunk of bread high above the breakfast table one morning, much to her parents' surprise.

These are true stories. There are many more of them. They are living proof that children who worship do so more observantly than we realize, and with a predisposition to bring home their learnings perhaps more readily than we adults!

Including children with the rest of God's family in public worship is a commitment worth making. A church that does so must be prepared to support that decision vigorously. If we do little more than abandon children to a primarily adult-defined worship hour, telling them only that they must "behave themselves" until they are "old enough to get something out of it," we nurture passivity, not worship, and we invite frustration all around. On the other hand, if we do too much to reinvent worship as a primarily child-centered experience, we make the mistake of neglecting the complex and often aching needs of adults to worship God in ways that are as intellectually rigorous as they are relevant to their daily struggles. Churches that are serious about children and adults worshiping together would do well to stake out a middle ground by making small but significant changes in the way worship happens so that children feel more included, and by finding more effective ways to teach children to participate meaningfully in the services as they are conducted in all their adult complexities.

A Children's Guide to Worship emerged out of the tumble of one church's efforts to do just that. In our congregation, children from age three through kindergarten attend the first fifteen minutes of the service, and beginning in the first grade, children remain with their parents for the entire service. We support this policy in a number of ways. We use a lectionary-based curriculum for church school so that, very often, children hear during worship the same biblical passages they studied earlier that morning. We offer an open house to introduce first graders and their parents to corporate worship, and we teach a special unit on communion to older children. We prepare children's worship folders, updated weekly not with busywork but with learning and listening activities. We identify specific roles children can play to share in worship leadership and we actively recruit children to fill these roles, for example as children's or youth choir members, ushers, greeters, Advent or Lent readers, candle lighters, or as participants in children's musicals and youth-led services.

In developing *A Children's Guide to Worship* we directed our attention to the needs of children in the pews who do not have specific leadership roles on any given Sunday. Our goal was to create a permanent, year-round resource for children to use by themselves, or together with an adult, to help them worship God with understanding. We envisioned a resource that would appeal to readers and nonreaders alike, targeting children from age three through third grade. We hoped the guide would remain in the pews as a supplement to the bulletin, Bible, and hymnal, and that it would draw children *into* worship, not distract them *from* worship. We also imagined families owning a copy of their own at home to stimulate conversation about God during the week. Last but certainly not least, we hoped that parents of young children would feel supported as they practiced, week after week, the vital skill of worshiping together as a family within the larger family of God.

When our Children's Ministry Committee first talked about developing such a resource, it was in the middle of one of our regular meetings. None of us had any inkling of the eventual outcome of this project, one among many pressing items of business that were crowding the agenda that night. Nevertheless, a sense of inevitability has presided over the growth of this piece into its present form, which occurred over a period of months in the creative interchange between writers and illustrator, between pastors and lay persons, between a worship committee and an education committee, between those who are parents of young children and those who are not. That this guide was developed in direct response both to the needs of real children, who fidget and squiggle by God's design, and to the needs of real parents, who wonder and worry by God's design, is, I believe, the very reason it appears to have found a wider readership.

All of us who worked on this project are indebted to Harold and Joan Williams for the original inspiration and for the means with which to make it happen. Additionally, we are indebted to David Ng and Virginia Thomas for their book *Children in the Worshiping Community*, which undergirds this present effort, as well as to the children, parents, and other caring adults of the Bedford Presbyterian Church for their faithfulness, to the Children's Ministry Committee of the Bedford Presbyterian Church for its vision and hard work over the years, to Marcia

Morgan and Morgan Press for their generosity in printing the first run, to Terry Tucker for counsel, to Kathy Metivier and Michelle Jones for ongoing support, and to LindaJo McKim and Geneva Press for enabling us to share our work more widely.

In pondering the finished piece, we found ourselves, as writers and illustrator, thinking of those who have nurtured us in our love for God and in our love for the worship of God. Collectively we acknowledge Robert and Jean Boling, Marge and Frank Dahle, William and Anna Warncke, and Katelynn and Molly Vance for showing us the way.

Above all, we are indebted to God who nurtures our spirits to want one thing before all others, and that is that we might glorify God, enjoying God, with all our hearts, our souls, our strength, and our minds forever. *A Children's Guide to Worship* is evidence of God's wise nurturing toward this end. Its purpose is to nurture others in like manner. We who co-conspired to bring it into being marvel that God has let us be in on the plan.

Ruth L. Boling

Bedford, New Hampshire
October 1996